for

from

I keep asking that the God of our Lord Jesus Christ, the glorious Father, may give you the Spirit of wisdom and revelation, so that you may know him better.

—Ephesians 1:17 (NIV)

Authentic Publishing
We welcome your questions and comments.

USA	1820 Jet Stream Drive, Colorado Springs, CO 80921 www.authenticbooks.com
UK	9 Holdom Avenue, Bletchley, Milton Keynes, Bucks, MK1 1QR www.authenticmedia.co.uk
India	Logos Bhavan, Medchal Road, Jeedimetla Village, Secunderabad 500 055, A.P.

God's Promises on Knowing Him
ISBN 978-1-934068-88-5

Livingstone project staff includes Andy Culbertson, Linda Taylor, Joan Guest, Everett O'Bryan. Interior design by Lindsay Galvin and Larry Taylor. Typeset by Kirk Luttrell.

Published in 2008 by Authentic.

A catalog record for this book is available from the Library of Congress.

13 12 11 10 09 08 / 1 2 3 4 5 6

Printed in the United States of America

GOD'S PROMISES

on Knowing Him

CONTENTS

Experiencing God

D'S PROMIS

ROM

OUR WONDERFUL *God*

Be still, and know that I am God; I will be exalted among the nations, I will be exalted in the earth.

—Psalm 46:10 (NIV)

ES GOD'S PROMISES GOD'S

The Presence OF GOD

Do what is good and run from evil so that you may live! Then the LORD God of Heaven's Armies will be your helper, just as you have claimed.

—Amos 5:14 (NLT)

He who dwells in the shelter of the Most High will rest in the shadow of the Almighty.

—Psalm 91:1 (NIV)

For the eyes of the LORD run to and fro throughout the whole earth, to show Himself strong on behalf of those whose heart is loyal to Him. In this you have done foolishly; therefore from now on you shall have wars.

—2 Chronicles 16:9 (NKJV)

Even if I walk through a valley as dark as the grave, I will not be afraid of any danger. Why? Because you are with me, Lord. Your rod and staff comfort me.

—Psalm 23:4 (ERV)

The Lord will guide you always; he will satisfy your needs in a sun-scorched land and will strengthen your frame. You will be like a well-watered garden, like a spring whose waters never fail.

—Isaiah 58:11 (NIV)

You will show me the path of life; in Your presence is fullness of joy; at Your right hand are pleasures forevermore.

—Psalm 16:11 (NKJV)

Don't be afraid, for I am with you. Don't be discouraged, for I am your God. I will strengthen you and help you. I will hold you up with my victorious right hand.

—Isaiah 41:10 (NLT)

Now may our Lord Jesus Christ himself and God our Father, who loved us and by his grace gave us eternal comfort and a wonderful hope, comfort you and strengthen you in every good thing you do and say.

—2 Thessalonians 2:16–17 (NLT)

I was innocent and you supported me. You let me stand and serve you forever.

—Psalm 41:12 (ERV)

The LORD replied, "My Presence will go with you, and I will give you rest."

—Exodus 33:14 (NIV)

You have endowed him with eternal blessings and given him the joy of your presence.

—Psalm 21:6 (NLT)

May he, as a result, make your hearts strong, blameless, and holy as you stand before God our Father when our Lord Jesus comes again with all his holy people. Amen.

—1 Thessalonians 3:13 (NLT)

The Power OF GOD

God is more powerful than any of your gods. The God of Israel makes his people strong.

—Psalm 68:34 (ERV)

The Lord raises his voice at the sea. The voice of the glorious God is like thunder over the great ocean. The Lord's voice shows his power. His voice shows his glory.

—Psalm 29:3–4 (ERV)

For since the creation of the world God's invisible qualities—his eternal power and divine nature—have been clearly seen, being understood from what has been made, so that men are without excuse.

—Romans 1:20 (NIV)

His divine power has given to us all things that pertain to life and godliness, through the knowledge of Him who called us by glory and virtue.

—2 Peter 1:3 (NKJV)

The message of the cross is foolish to those who are headed for destruction! But we who are being saved know it is the very power of God.

—1 Corinthians 1:18 (NLT)

The Lord thundered from heaven; the voice of the Most High resounded amid the hail and burning coals. . . . He reached down from heaven and rescued me; he drew me out of deep waters. He rescued me from my powerful enemies, from those who hated me and were too strong for me.

—Psalm 18:13, 16–17 (NLT)

My message and my preaching were not with wise and persuasive words, but with a demonstration of the Spirit's power, so that your faith might not rest on men's wisdom, but on God's power.

—1 Corinthians 2:4–5 (NIV)

Blessed be the God and Father of our Lord Jesus Christ, who according to His abundant mercy has begotten us again to a living hope through the resurrection of Jesus Christ from the dead, to an inheritance incorruptible and undefiled and that does not fade away, reserved in heaven for you, who are kept by the power of God through faith for salvation ready to be revealed in the last time.

—1 Peter 1:3–5 (NKJV)

I will meditate on all your works and consider all your mighty deeds.

—Psalm 77:12 (NIV)

I am the Lord; there is no other God. I have equipped you for battle, though you don't even know me, so all the world from east to west will know there is no other God. I am the Lord, and there is no other.

—Isaiah 45:5–6 (NLT)

God, if I am in trouble, keep me alive. If my enemies are angry at me, save me from them.

—Psalm 138:7 (ERV)

Now all glory to God, who is able to keep you from falling away and will bring you with great joy into his glorious presence without a single fault. All glory to him who alone is God, our Savior through Jesus Christ our Lord. All glory, majesty, power, and authority are his before all time, and in the present, and beyond all time! Amen.

—Jude 24–25 (NLT)

You answer us with awesome deeds of righteousness, O God our Savior, the hope of all the ends of the earth and of the farthest seas, who formed the mountains by your power, having armed yourself with strength, who stilled the roaring of the seas, the roaring of their waves, and the turmoil of the nations.

—Psalm 65:5–7 (NIV)

But let all those rejoice who put their trust in You; let them ever shout for joy, because You defend them; let those also who love Your name be joyful in You.

—Psalm 5:11 (NKJV)

Even the foolishness of God is wiser than human wisdom. Even the weakness of God is stronger than human strength.

—1 Corinthians 1:25 (ERV)

For I am persuaded that neither death nor life, nor angels nor principalities nor powers, nor things present nor things to come, nor height nor depth, nor any other created thing, shall be able to separate us from the love of God which is in Christ Jesus our Lord.

—Romans 8:38–39 (NKJV)

You are my hiding place; you will protect me from trouble and surround me with songs of deliverance.

—Psalm 32:7 (NIV)

And God will generously provide all you need. Then you will always have everything you need and plenty left over to share with others.

—2 Corinthians 9:8 (NLT)

Wherever I am, however weak, I will call to you for help! Carry me to the place of safety far above.

—Psalm 61:2 (ERV)

I am not ashamed of the gospel, because it is the power of God for the salvation of everyone who believes: first for the Jew, then for the Gentile.

—Romans 1:16 (NIV)

Who is this King of glory? The LORD strong and mighty, the LORD mighty in battle.

—Psalm 24:8 (NKJV)

You want proof that Christ is speaking through me. My proof is that Christ is not weak in punishing you. But Christ is powerful among you. It is true that Christ was weak when he was killed on the cross. But he lives now by God's power. And it is true that we are weak in Christ. But for you we will be alive in Christ by God's power.

—2 Corinthians 13:3–4 (ERV)

The Nearness OF GOD

The LORD is close to all who call on him, yes, to all who call on him in truth.

—Psalm 145:18 (NLT)

Let us draw near to God with a sincere heart in full assurance of faith, having our hearts sprinkled to cleanse us from a guilty conscience and having our bodies washed with pure water.

—Hebrews 10:22 (NIV)

Come near to God and he will come near to you. Wash your hands, you sinners, and purify your hearts, you double-minded.

—James 4:8 (NIV)

Lawless people are coming to attack me; they live far from your instructions.

—Psalm 119:150 (NLT)

The Lord our God is near when we ask him to help us. No other nation has a god like that!

—Deuteronomy 4:7 (ERV)

Be not far from Me, for trouble is near; for there is none to help.

—Psalm 22:11 (NKJV)

But as for me, how good it is to be near God! I have made the Sovereign LORD my shelter, and I will tell everyone about the wonderful things you do.

—Psalm 73:28 (NLT)

Surely his salvation is near those who fear him, that his glory may dwell in our land.

—Psalm 85:9 (NIV)

Draw near to my soul, and redeem it; deliver me because of my enemies.

—Psalm 69:18 (NKJV)

And may these words that I have prayed in the presence of the LORD be before him constantly, day and night, so that the LORD our God may give justice to me and to his people Israel, according to each day's needs. Then people all over the earth will know that the LORD alone is God and there is no other.

—1 Kings 8:59–60 (NLT)

So you should look for the Lord before it is too late. You should call to him now, while he is near.

—Isaiah 55:6 (ERV)

Lord All-Powerful, my King, my God, even the birds have found a home in your temple. They make their nests near your altar. And there they have their babies.

—Psalm 84:3 (ERV)

May the LORD our God be with us as he was with our fathers; may he never leave us nor forsake us. May he turn our hearts to him, to walk in all his ways and to keep the commands, decrees and regulations he gave our fathers. And may these words of mine, which I have prayed before the LORD, be near to the LORD our God day and night, that he may uphold the cause of his servant and the cause of his people Israel according to each day's need, so that all the peoples of the earth may know that the LORD is God and that there is no other. But your hearts must be fully committed to the LORD our God, to live by his decrees and obey his commands, as at this time.

—1 Kings 8:57–61 (NIV)

Let your gentleness be known to all men. The Lord is at hand.

—Philippians 4:5 (NKJV)

We thank you, O God! We give thanks because you are near. People everywhere tell of your wonderful deeds.

—Psalm 75:1 (NLT)

But now in Christ Jesus you who once were far off have been brought near by the blood of Christ.

—Ephesians 2:13 (NKJV)

You came near when I called you, and you said, "Do not fear." O Lord, you took up my case; you redeemed my life.

—Lamentations 3:57–58 (NIV)

Blessed are those you choose and bring near to live in your courts! We are filled with the good things of your house, of your holy temple.

—Psalm 65:4 (NIV)

The Abundance OF GOD

From his abundance we have all received one gracious blessing after another.

—John 1:16 (NLT)

Nevertheless, I will bring health and healing to it; I will heal my people and will let them enjoy abundant peace and security.

—Jeremiah 33:6 (NIV)

For if by the one man's offense death reigned through the one, much more those who receive abundance of grace and of the gift of righteousness will reign in life through the One, Jesus Christ.

—Romans 5:17 (NKJV)

Behold, God is great, and we do not know Him; nor can the number of His years be discovered. For He draws up drops of water, which distill as rain from the mist, which the clouds drop down and pour abundantly on man.

—Job 36:26–28 (NKJV)

Now these are the gifts Christ gave to the church: the apostles, the prophets, the evangelists, and the pastors and teachers. Their responsibility is to equip God's people to do his work and build up the church, the body of Christ. This will continue until we all come to such unity in our faith and knowledge of God's Son that we will be mature in the Lord, measuring up to the full and complete standard of Christ.

—Ephesians 4:11–13 (NLT)

Grace (kindness) and peace be given to you more and more, because now you know God and Jesus our Lord.

—2 Peter 1:2 (ERV)

No person can understand how God spreads the clouds out or how the thunder rumbles in the sky. Look, God spread the lightning over the earth and covered the deepest part of the ocean. God uses them to control the nations and to give them plenty of food.

—Job 36:29–31 (ERV)

They shall utter the memory of Your great goodness, and shall sing of Your righteousness.

—Psalm 145:7 (NKJV)

I will bless her with abundant provisions; her poor will I satisfy with food.

—Psalm 132:15 (NIV)

[I pray] that Christ may dwell in your hearts through faith; that you, being rooted and grounded in love, may be able to comprehend with all the saints what is the width and length and depth and height—to know the love of Christ which passes knowledge; that you may be filled with all the fullness of God.

—Ephesians 3:17–19 (NKJV)

And God will generously provide all you need. Then you will always have everything you need and plenty left over to share with others.

—2 Corinthians 9:8 (NLT)

For in Christ lives all the fullness of God in a human body. So you also are complete through your union with Christ, who is the head over every ruler and authority.

—Colossians 2:9–10 (NLT)

You sent abundant rain, O God, to refresh the weary land.

—Psalm 68:9 (NLT)

For it pleased the Father that in Him all the fullness should dwell, and by Him to reconcile all things to Himself, by Him, whether things on earth or things in heaven, having made peace through the blood of His cross.

—Colossians 1:19–20 (NKJV)

"I will give the priests plenty of food. And my people will be filled and satisfied with the good things I give them." This message is from the Lord.

—Jeremiah 31:14 (ERV)

Be glad, O people of Zion, rejoice in the LORD your God, for he has given you the autumn rains in righteousness. He sends you abundant showers, both autumn and spring rains, as before.

—Joel 2:23 (NIV)

Then Jesus said to his disciples: "Therefore I tell you, do not worry about your life, what you will eat; or about your body, what you will wear. Life is more than food, and the body more than clothes. Consider the ravens: They do not sow or reap, they have no storeroom or barn; yet God feeds them. And how much more valuable you are than birds! . . . But seek his kingdom, and these things will be given to you as well."

—Luke 12:22–24, 31 (NIV)

The Love OF GOD

We have known and believed the love that God has for us. God is love, and he who abides in love abides in God, and God in him.

—1 John 4:16 (NKJV)

The Father (God) has loved us so much! This shows how much he loved us: We are called children of God. And we really are God's children. But the people in the world (people who don't believe) don't understand that we are God's children, because they have not known him (God).

—1 John 3:1 (ERV)

For as the heavens are high above the earth, so great is His mercy toward those who fear Him.

—Psalm 103:11 (NKJV)

God showed how much he loved us by sending his one and only Son into the world so that we might have eternal life through him.

—1 John 4:9 (NLT)

There is no fear in love. But perfect love drives out fear, because fear has to do with punishment. The one who fears is not made perfect in love.

—1 John 4:18 (NIV)

The LORD has appeared of old to me, saying: "Yes, I have loved you with an everlasting love; therefore with lovingkindness I have drawn you."

—Jeremiah 31:3 (NKJV)

Yes, God loved the world so much that he gave his only Son. God gave his Son so that every person that believes in him would not be lost, but have life forever.

—John 3:16 (ERV)

But from everlasting to everlasting the LORD'S love is with those who fear him, and his righteousness with their children's children.

—Psalm 103:17 (NIV)

Lord, your true love is higher than the sky. Your loyalty is higher than the clouds.

—Psalm 36:5 (ERV)

But God's mercy is very great, and God loved us very much. We were spiritually dead. We were dead because of the things we did wrong against God. But God gave us new life with Christ. You have been saved by God's grace (kindness).

—Ephesians 2:4–5 (ERV)

This is real love—not that we loved God, but that he loved us and sent his Son as a sacrifice to take away our sins.

—1 John 4:10 (NLT)

"For the mountains may move and the hills disappear, but even then my faithful love for you will remain. My covenant of blessing will never be broken," says the LORD, who has mercy on you.

—Isaiah 54:10 (NLT)

But God demonstrates his own love for us in this: While we were still sinners, Christ died for us.

—Romans 5:8 (NIV)

We love because God first loved us.

—1 John 4:19 (ERV)

The Goodness OF GOD

Now therefore, arise, O LORD God, to Your resting place, You and the ark of Your strength. Let Your priests, O LORD God, be clothed with salvation, and let Your saints rejoice in goodness.

—2 Chronicles 6:41 (NKJV)

The LORD is good to all, and His tender mercies are over all His works.

—Psalm 145:9 (NKJV)

The LORD is good, a strong refuge when trouble comes. He is close to those who trust in him.

—Nahum 1:7 (NLT)

Because of the LORD'S great love we are not consumed, for his compassions never fail. They are new every morning; great is your faithfulness.

—Lamentations 3:22–23 (NIV)

The Lord is our protector and glorious king. God blesses us with kindness and glory. The Lord gives every good thing to people who follow and obey him.

—Psalm 84:11 (ERV)

"Why do you call me good?" Jesus answered. "No one is good—except God alone."

—Mark 10:18 (NIV)

Dear friend, don't let this bad example influence you. Follow only what is good. Remember that those who do good prove that they are God's children, and those who do evil prove that they do not know God.

—3 John 11 (NLT)

Oh, give thanks to the LORD, for He is good! For His mercy endures forever.

—1 Chronicles 16:34 (NKJV)

Many are asking, "Who can show us any good?" Let the light of your face shine upon us, O LORD.

—Psalm 4:6 (NIV)

I sing a happy song to the Lord because he did good things for me.

—Psalm 13:6 (ERV)

I said to the LORD, "You are my Master! Every good thing I have comes from you."

—Psalm 16:2 (NLT)

Do not remember the rebellious sins of my youth. Remember me in the light of your unfailing love, for you are merciful, O LORD. The LORD is good and does what is right; he shows the proper path to those who go astray.

—Psalm 25:7–8 (NLT)

I am still confident of this: I will see the goodness of the Lord in the land of the living.

—Psalm 27:13 (NIV)

Oh, taste and see that the Lord is good; blessed is the man who trusts in Him!

—Psalm 34:8 (NKJV)

Lord, your love is good. Answer me with all your love. With all your kindness, turn to me and help me!

—Psalm 69:16 (ERV)

"The Lord is my portion," says my soul, "therefore I hope in Him!" The Lord is good to those who wait for Him, to the soul who seeks Him.

—Lamentations 3:24–25 (NKJV)

You are forgiving and good, O Lord, abounding in love to all who call to you.

—Psalm 86:5 (NIV)

Send me a sign of your favor. Then those who hate me will be put to shame, for you, O LORD, help and comfort me.

—Psalm 86:17 (NLT)

The Lord is good! His love is forever. We can trust him forever and ever!

—Psalm 100:5 (ERV)

But You, O GOD the Lord, deal with me for Your name's sake; because Your mercy is good, deliver me.

—Psalm 109:21 (NKJV)

Praise the LORD, for the LORD is good; celebrate his lovely name with music.

—Psalm 135:3 (NLT)

Oh, how great is Your goodness, which You have laid up for those who fear You, which You have prepared for those who trust in You in the presence of the sons of men!

—Psalm 31:19 (NKJV)

I will tell of the kindnesses of the LORD, the deeds for which he is to be praised, according to all the LORD has done for us—yes, the many good things he has done for the house of Israel, according to his compassion and many kindnesses.

—Isaiah 63:7 (NIV)

What can I give to the Lord? The Lord gave me everything I have!

—Psalm 116:12 (ERV)

They will celebrate your abundant goodness and joyfully sing of your righteousness.

—Psalm 145:7 (NIV)

Behold what manner of love the Father has bestowed on us, that we should be called children of God! Therefore the world does not know us, because it did not know Him.

—1 John 3:1 (NKJV)

"There will be sounds of joy and happiness. There will be the happy sounds of a bride and groom. There will be the sounds of people bringing their gifts to the Lord's temple. Those people will say, 'Praise the Lord All-Powerful! The Lord is good! The Lord's kindness continues forever!' The people will say these things because I will again do good things to Judah. It will be like in the beginning." The Lord said these things.

—Jeremiah 33:11 (ERV)

By his divine power, God has given us everything we need for living a godly life. We have received all of this by coming to know him, the one who called us to himself by means of his marvelous glory and excellence.

—2 Peter 1:3 (NLT)

God, you are good, and you do good things. Teach me your laws.
—Psalm 119:68 (ERV)

God saw all that he had made, and it was very good. And there was evening, and there was morning—the sixth day.
—Genesis 1:31 (NIV)

The Sovereignty OF GOD

Your throne, O LORD, has stood from time immemorial. You yourself are from the everlasting past.

—Psalm 93:2 (NLT)

Lord God All-Powerful, there is no one like you. We can trust you completely. You proudly rule the sea. You can calm its angry waves.

—Psalm 89:8–9 (ERV)

And we know that all things work together for good to those who love God, to those who are the called according to His purpose.

—Romans 8:28 (NKJV)

He is our God. He is the God that saves us. The Lord our God saves us from death.

—Psalm 68:20 (ERV)

For it is God who works in you to will and to act according to his good purpose.

—Philippians 2:13 (NIV)

He prayed, "O Lord, God of our ancestors, you alone are the God who is in heaven. You are ruler of all the kingdoms of the earth. You are powerful and mighty; no one can stand against you!"

—2 Chronicles 20:6 (NLT)

My Master, you are my hope. I have trusted you since I was a young boy.

—Psalm 71:5 (ERV)

There are many plans in a man's heart, nevertheless the LORD'S counsel—that will stand.

—Proverbs 19:21 (NKJV)

Your throne, O God, will last for ever and ever; a scepter of justice will be the scepter of your kingdom.

—Psalm 45:6 (NIV)

God sits on his holy throne. God rules all the nations.

—Psalm 47:8 (ERV)

He will swallow up death forever! The Sovereign LORD will wipe away all tears. He will remove forever all insults and mockery against his land and people. The LORD has spoken!

—Isaiah 25:8 (NLT)

But it is good for me to draw near to God; I have put my trust in the Lord GOD, that I may declare all Your works.

—Psalm 73:28 (NKJV)

The Lord is in his holy palace. The Lord sits on his throne in heaven. And he sees everything that happens. The Lord watches people closely to see if they are good or bad.

—Psalm 11:4 (ERV)

May the nations be glad and sing for joy, for you rule the peoples justly and guide the nations of the earth.

—Psalm 67:4 (NIV)

The Lord has made the heavens his throne; from there he rules over everything.

—Psalm 103:19 (NLT)

Then God's special people will rule the kingdom. And they will rule over all the people from all the kingdoms of earth. This kingdom will last forever. And people from all the other kingdoms will respect and serve them.

—Daniel 7:27 (ERV)

So when they heard that, they raised their voice to God with one accord and said: "Lord, You are God, who made heaven and earth and the sea, and all that is in them."

—Acts 4:24 (NKJV)

"For I know the plans I have for you," says the LORD. "They are plans for good and not for disaster, to give you a future and a hope."

—Jeremiah 29:11 (NLT)

The LORD frustrates the plans of the nations and thwarts all their schemes. But the LORD's plans stand firm forever; his intentions can never be shaken.

—Psalm 33:10–11 (NLT)

In his heart a man plans his course, but the LORD determines his steps.

—Proverbs 16:9 (NIV)

God rules the world with his great power. God watches people everywhere. No person can rebel against him.

—Psalm 66:7 (ERV)

I lift my eyes to you, O God, enthroned in heaven.

—Psalm 123:1 (NLT)

All the ends of the earth will remember and turn to the Lord, and all the families of the nations will bow down before him, for dominion belongs to the Lord and he rules over the nations.

—Psalm 22:27–28 (NIV)

But my eyes are upon You, O God the Lord; in You I take refuge; do not leave my soul destitute.

—Psalm 141:8 (NKJV)

The Lord my Master is coming with power. He will use his power to rule all the people. The Lord will bring rewards for his people. He will have their payment with him. The Lord will lead his people like a shepherd leads sheep. The Lord will use his arm (power) and gather his sheep together. The Lord will pick up the little sheep and hold them in his arms. Their mothers will walk beside him.

—Isaiah 40:10–11 (ERV)

Lord my Master, I am your servant. I know that you have shown me only a small part of the wonderful and powerful things you will do. There is no god in heaven or earth that can do the great and powerful things you have done!

—Deuteronomy 3:24 (ERV)

The Spirit OF GOD GIVES LIFE

The Spirit of God has made me; the breath of the Almighty gives me life.
—Job 33:4 (NIV)

In Him you also trusted, after you heard the word of truth, the gospel of your salvation; in whom also, having believed, you were sealed with the Holy Spirit of promise, who is the guarantee of our inheritance until the redemption of the purchased possession, to the praise of His glory.
—Ephesians 1:13–14 (NKJV)

The Spirit Himself bears witness with our spirit that we are children of God.
—Romans 8:16 (NKJV)

When God our Savior revealed his kindness and love, he saved us, not because of the righteous things we had done, but because of his mercy. He washed away our sins, giving us a new birth and new life through the Holy Spirit.

—Titus 3:4–5 (NLT)

But Jesus answered, "I tell you the truth. A person must be born from water and the Spirit. If a person is not born from water and the Spirit, then he cannot enter God's kingdom. A person's body is born from his human parents. But a person's spiritual life is born from the Spirit."

—John 3:5–6 (ERV)

The mind of sinful man is death, but the mind controlled by the Spirit is life and peace.

—Romans 8:6 (NIV)

The Spirit alone gives eternal life. Human effort accomplishes nothing. And the very words I have spoken to you are spirit and life.

—John 6:63 (NLT)

God raised Jesus from death. And if God's Spirit is living in you, then he will also give life to your bodies that die. God is the One who raised Christ from death. And he will give life to your bodies through his Spirit that lives in you.

—Romans 8:11 (ERV)

However, as it is written: "No eye has seen, no ear has heard, no mind has conceived what God has prepared for those who love him"—but God has revealed it to us by his Spirit. The Spirit searches all things, even the deep things of God.

—1 Corinthians 2:9–10 (NIV)

For the kingdom of God is not eating and drinking, but righteousness and peace and joy in the Holy Spirit.

—Romans 14:17 (NKJV)

And because we are his children, God has sent the Spirit of his Son into our hearts, prompting us to call out, "Abba, Father." Now you are no longer a slave but God's own child. And since you are his child, God has made you his heir.

—Galatians 4:6–7 (NLT)

No one has seen God at any time. If we love one another, God abides in us, and His love has been perfected in us. By this we know that we abide in Him, and He in us, because He has given us of His Spirit.

—1 John 4:12–13 (NKJV)

If a person plants (lives) to satisfy his sinful self, then his sinful self will bring him eternal death. But if a person plants to please the Spirit, he will get eternal life from the Spirit.

—Galatians 6:8 (ERV)

For the Lord is the Spirit, and wherever the Spirit of the Lord is, there is freedom.

—2 Corinthians 3:17 (NLT)

Don't you know that you yourselves are God's temple and that God's Spirit lives in you?

—1 Corinthians 3:16 (NIV)

If we live in the Spirit, let us also walk in the Spirit.

—Galatians 5:25 (NKJV)

This means that anyone who belongs to Christ has become a new person. The old life is gone; a new life has begun!

—2 Corinthians 5:17 (NLT)

When people sin, they earn what sin pays—death. But God gives his people a free gift—life forever in Christ Jesus our Lord.

—Romans 6:23 (ERV)

So brothers and sisters, I beg you to do something. God has shown us great mercy. So offer your lives as a living sacrifice to God. Your offering must be only for God and will be pleasing to him. This offering of yourselves is the spiritual way for you to worship (serve) God. Don't change yourselves to be like the people of this world. But let God change you inside with a new way of thinking. Then you will be able to decide and accept what God wants for you. You will be able to know what things are good and pleasing to God and what things are perfect.

—Romans 12:1–2 (ERV)

The Spirit OF GOD GIVES UNDERSTANDING

Now we have received, not the spirit of the world, but the Spirit who is from God, that we might know the things that have been freely given to us by God.

—1 Corinthians 2:12 (NKJV)

I am telling you these things now while I am still with you. But when the Father sends the Advocate as my representative—that is, the Holy Spirit—he will teach you everything and will remind you of everything I have told you.

—John 14:25–26 (NLT)

Now hope does not disappoint, because the love of God has been poured out in our hearts by the Holy Spirit who was given to us.

—Romans 5:5 (NKJV)

And the Holy Spirit helps us in our weakness. For example, we don't know what God wants us to pray for. But the Holy Spirit prays for us with groanings that cannot be expressed in words.

—Romans 8:26 (NLT)

And I will ask the Father, and he will give you another Counselor to be with you forever—the Spirit of truth. The world cannot accept him, because it neither sees him nor knows him. But you know him, for he lives with you and will be in you.

—John 14:16–17 (NIV)

Teach me to do your will, for you are my God; may your good Spirit lead me on level ground.

—Psalm 143:10 (NIV)

Now when they bring you to the synagogues and magistrates and authorities, do not worry about how or what you should answer, or what you should say. For the Holy Spirit will teach you in that very hour what you ought to say.

—Luke 12:11–12 (NKJV)

And I will put my Spirit inside you. I will change you so you will obey my laws. You will carefully obey my commands.

—Ezekiel 36:27 (ERV)

If you then, though you are evil, know how to give good gifts to your children, how much more will your Father in heaven give the Holy Spirit to those who ask him!

—Luke 11:13 (NIV)

However, when He, the Spirit of truth, has come, He will guide you into all truth; for He will not speak on His own authority, but whatever He hears He will speak; and He will tell you things to come.

—John 16:13 (NKJV)

Those who are dominated by the sinful nature think about sinful things, but those who are controlled by the Holy Spirit think about things that please the Spirit.

—Romans 8:5 (NLT)

When the Counselor comes, whom I will send to you from the Father, the Spirit of truth who goes out from the Father, he will testify about me.

—John 15:26 (NIV)

But in fact, it is best for you that I go away, because if I don't, the Advocate won't come. If I do go away, then I will send him to you. And when he comes, he will convict the world of its sin, and of God's righteousness, and of the coming judgment.

—John 16:7–8 (NLT)

I pray that the God who gives hope will fill you with much joy and peace while you trust in him. Then you will have more and more hope, and it will flow out of you by the power of the Holy Spirit.

—Romans 15:13 (ERV)

All things that the Father has are Mine. Therefore I said that He will take of Mine and declare it to you.

—John 16:15 (NKJV)

Grace (kindness) and peace be given to you more and more, because now you know God and Jesus our Lord. Jesus has the power of God. And his power has given us everything we need to live and to serve God. We have these things because we know him. Jesus called us by his glory and goodness.

—2 Peter 1:2–3 (ERV)

I keep asking that the God of our Lord Jesus Christ, the glorious Father, may give you the Spirit of wisdom and revelation, so that you may know him better.

—Ephesians 1:17 (NIV)

For the Lord is the Spirit, and wherever the Spirit of the Lord is, there is freedom.

—2 Corinthians 3:17 (NLT)

God can see what is in people's hearts. And God knows what is in the mind of the Spirit, because the Spirit speaks to God for his people in the way that God wants.

—Romans 8:27 (ERV)

I want them to be strengthened and joined together with love. I want them to have the full confidence that comes from understanding. I mean I want them to know fully the secret truth that God has made known. That truth is Christ himself. In Christ all the treasures of wisdom and knowledge are safely kept. I tell you these things so that no person can fool you by telling you ideas that seem good, but are false. I am not there with you, but my heart is with you. I am happy to see your good lives and your strong faith in Christ.

—Colossians 2:2–5 (ERV)

D'S PROMIS

ROM

KNOWING

God

I pray that out of his glorious riches he may strengthen you with power through his Spirit in your inner being, so that Christ may dwell in your hearts through faith. And I pray that you, being rooted and established in love, may have power, together with all the saints, to grasp how wide and long and high and deep is the love of Christ, and to know this love that surpasses knowledge—that you may be filled to the measure of all the fullness of God.

—Ephesians 3:16–19 (NIV)

Jesus answered, "I am the way and the truth and the life. No one comes to the Father except through me."

—John 14:6 (NIV)

Let not your heart be troubled; you believe in God, believe also in Me.

—John 14:1 (NKJV)

When you were dead in your sins and in the uncircumcision of your sinful nature, God made you alive with Christ. He forgave us all our sins, having canceled the written code, with its regulations, that was against us and that stood opposed to us; he took it away, nailing it to the cross.

—Colossians 2:13–14 (NIV)

This means that anyone who belongs to Christ has become a new person. The old life is gone; a new life has begun! And all of this is a gift from God, who brought us back to himself through Christ. And God has given us this task of reconciling people to him.

—2 Corinthians 5:17–18 (NLT)

If you keep My commandments, you will abide in My love, just as I have kept My Father's commandments and abide in His love. These things I have spoken to you, that My joy may remain in you, and that your joy may be full.

—John 15:10–11 (NKJV)

Therefore, there is now no condemnation for those who are in Christ Jesus, because through Christ Jesus the law of the Spirit of life set me free from the law of sin and death.

—Romans 8:1–2 (NIV)

My Father has entrusted everything to me. No one truly knows the Son except the Father, and no one truly knows the Father except the Son and those to whom the Son chooses to reveal him.

—Luke 10:22 (NLT)

We should always follow the example of Jesus. Jesus is the leader in our faith. And he makes our faith perfect. He suffered death on the cross. But Jesus accepted the shame of the cross like it was nothing. He did this because of the joy that God put before him. And now he is sitting at the right side of God's throne. Think about Jesus. He was patient while sinful men were doing bad things against him. Think about him, so that you also will be patient and not stop trying.

—Hebrews 12:2–3 (ERV)

After saying all these things, Jesus looked up to heaven and said, "Father, the hour has come. Glorify your Son so he can give glory back to you. For you have given him authority over everyone. He gives eternal life to each one you have given him. And this is the way to have eternal life—to know you, the only true God, and Jesus Christ, the one you sent to earth. I brought glory to you here on earth by completing the work you gave me to do. Now, Father, bring me into the glory we shared before the world began."

—John 17:1–5 (NLT)

Knowing God THROUGH HIS FORGIVENESS

Godly sorrow brings repentance that leads to salvation and leaves no regret, but worldly sorrow brings death.

—2 Corinthians 7:10 (NIV)

Then if my people who are called by my name will humble themselves and pray and seek my face and turn from their wicked ways, I will hear from heaven and will forgive their sins and restore their land.

—2 Chronicles 7:14 (NLT)

Let us know, let us pursue the knowledge of the LORD. His going forth is established as the morning; He will come to us like the rain, like the latter and former rain to the earth.

—Hosea 6:3 (NKJV)

But Job, you should make your heart ready to serve only God, and you should lift up your hands to worship him. You should put away the sin that is in your home. Don't let evil live in your tent. Then you could look to God without shame. You could stand strong and not be afraid.

—Job 11:13–15 (ERV)

Peter replied, "Repent and be baptized, every one of you, in the name of Jesus Christ for the forgiveness of your sins. And you will receive the gift of the Holy Spirit."

—Acts 2:38 (NIV)

Now repent of your sins and turn to God, so that your sins may be wiped away.

—Acts 3:19 (NLT)

In fact, it says, "The message is very close at hand; it is on your lips and in your heart." And that message is the very message about faith that we preach: If you confess with your mouth that Jesus is Lord and believe in your heart that God raised him from the dead, you will be saved.

—Romans 10:8–9 (NLT)

If we confess our sins, He is faithful and just to forgive us our sins and to cleanse us from all unrighteousness.

—1 John 1:9 (NKJV)

Praise be to the God and Father of our Lord Jesus Christ. God has great mercy, and because of his mercy he gave us a new life. This new life brings us a living hope through Jesus Christ's rising from death.

—1 Peter 1:3 (ERV)

Lord, you are the God we can trust. I put my life in your hands. Save me!

—Psalm 31:5 (ERV)

For troubles without number surround me; my sins have overtaken me, and I cannot see. They are more than the hairs of my head, and my heart fails within me. Be pleased, O LORD, to save me; O LORD, come quickly to help me.

—Psalm 40:12–13 (NIV)

Purify me from my sins, and I will be clean; wash me, and I will be whiter than snow.

—Psalm 51:7 (NLT)

Knowing God BY SEARCHING FOR HIM

My son, accept these things I say. Remember my commands. Listen to wisdom, and try your best to understand. Cry out for wisdom, and shout for understanding. Look for wisdom like silver. Look for it like a hidden treasure. If you do these things, then you will learn to respect the Lord. You will truly learn about God.

—Proverbs 2:1–5 (ERV)

I will give you a new heart and put a new spirit in you; I will remove from you your heart of stone and give you a heart of flesh.

—Ezekiel 36:26 (NIV)

And He has made from one blood every nation of men to dwell on all the face of the earth, and has determined their preappointed times and the boundaries of their dwellings, so that they should seek the Lord, in the hope that they might grope for Him and find Him, though He is not far from each one of us.

—Acts 17:26–27 (NKJV)

Your help made me so happy! Give me that joy again. Make my spirit strong and ready to obey you.

—Psalm 51:12 (ERV)

Do not remember the rebellious sins of my youth. Remember me in the light of your unfailing love, for you are merciful, O LORD.

—Psalm 25:7 (NLT)

Create in me a clean heart, O God, and renew a steadfast spirit within me.

—Psalm 51:10 (NKJV)

But seek first his kingdom and his righteousness, and all these things will be given to you as well.

—Matthew 6:33 (NIV)

Wash me clean from my guilt. Purify me from my sin.

—Psalm 51:2 (NLT)

The Lord looked down from heaven to see if there were any wise people. (Wise people turn to God for help.)

—Psalm 14:2 (ERV)

And we pray this in order that you may live a life worthy of the Lord and may please him in every way: bearing fruit in every good work, growing in the knowledge of God.

—Colossians 1:10 (NIV)

As the deer pants for the water brooks, so pants my soul for You, O God.

—Psalm 42:1 (NKJV)

Yes, God's riches are very great! God's wisdom and knowledge have no end! No person can explain the things God decides. No person can understand God's ways.

—Romans 11:33 (ERV)

If you look for me wholeheartedly, you will find me.

—Jeremiah 29:13 (NLT)

Grace and peace be multiplied to you in the knowledge of God and of Jesus our Lord.

—2 Peter 1:2 (NKJV)

I want to know Christ and the power of his resurrection and the fellowship of sharing in his sufferings, becoming like him in his death.

—Philippians 3:10 (NIV)

God, you are my God. And I want you so much. My soul and my body thirst for you, like a dry, weary land with no water. Yes, I have seen you in your temple. I have seen your strength and glory.

—Psalm 63:1–2 (ERV)

Search me, O God, and know my heart; test me and know my anxious thoughts. See if there is any offensive way in me, and lead me in the way everlasting.

—Psalm 139:23–24 (NIV)

But I, the LORD, search all hearts and examine secret motives. I give all people their due rewards, according to what their actions deserve.

—Jeremiah 17:10 (NLT)

Knowing God BY HOPING FOR HIM

Israel, trust the Lord. Trust him now, and trust him forever!

—Psalm 131:3 (ERV)

Let integrity and uprightness preserve me, for I wait for You.

—Psalm 25:21 (NKJV)

Young men become tired and need to rest. Even young boys stumble and fall. But people that trust the Lord become strong again like eagles that grow new feathers. These people run without becoming weak. These people walk without becoming tired.

—Isaiah 40:30–31 (ERV)

I will praise you forever, O God, for what you have done. I will trust in your good name in the presence of your faithful people.

—Psalm 52:9 (NLT)

Be strong and take heart, all you who hope in the LORD.

—Psalm 31:24 (NIV)

But the LORD watches over those who fear him, those who rely on his unfailing love. He rescues them from death and keeps them alive in times of famine.

—Psalm 33:18–19 (NLT)

The LORD is good to those who depend on him, to those who search for him. So it is good to wait quietly for salvation from the LORD.

—Lamentations 3:25–26 (NLT)

Why are you cast down, O my soul? And why are you disquieted within me? Hope in God, for I shall yet praise Him for the help of His countenance. O my God, my soul is cast down within me; therefore I will remember You from the land of the Jordan, and from the heights of Hermon, from the Hill Mizar.

—Psalm 42:5–6 (NKJV)

My soul faints for Your salvation, but I hope in Your word.

—Psalm 119:81 (NKJV)

I am waiting for the Lord to help me. My soul waits for him. I trust what the Lord says.

—Psalm 130:5 (ERV)

No one who trusts in you will ever be disgraced, but disgrace comes to those who try to deceive others.

—Psalm 25:3 (NLT)

Let Your mercy, O LORD, be upon us, just as we hope in You.

—Psalm 33:22 (NKJV)

O Israel, put your hope in the LORD, for with the LORD is unfailing love and with him is full redemption.

—Psalm 130:7 (NIV)

When we pray to God our Father we always thank him for the things you have done because of your faith. And we thank him for the work you have done because of your love. And we thank him that you continue to be strong because of your hope in our Lord Jesus Christ.

—1 Thessalonians 1:3 (ERV)

For evildoers shall be cut off; but those who wait on the LORD, They shall inherit the earth.

—Psalm 37:9 (NKJV)

And so, Lord, where do I put my hope?
My only hope is in you.

—Psalm 39:7 (NLT)

Through him you believe in God, who raised him from the dead and glorified him, and so your faith and hope are in God.

—1 Peter 1:21 (NIV)

Command those who are rich in this present age not to be haughty, nor to trust in uncertain riches but in the living God, who gives us richly all things to enjoy.

—1 Timothy 6:17 (NKJV)

Blessed is he whose help is the God of Jacob, whose hope is in the Lord his God, the Maker of heaven and earth, the sea, and everything in them—the Lord, who remains faithful forever.

—Psalm 146:5–6 (NIV)

I got up early in the morning to pray to you. I trust the things you say.

—Psalm 119:147 (ERV)

This is a faithful saying and worthy of all acceptance. For to this end we both labor and suffer reproach, because we trust in the living God, who is the Savior of all men, especially of those who believe.

—1 Timothy 4:9–10 (NKJV)

Knowing God BRINGS LIFE

Bless the LORD, O my soul, and forget not all His benefits: Who forgives all your iniquities, who heals all your diseases, who redeems your life from destruction, who crowns you with lovingkindness and tender mercies.

—Psalm 103:2–4 (NKJV)

But God's mercy is very great, and God loved us very much. We were spiritually dead. We were dead because of the things we did wrong against God. But God gave us new life with Christ. You have been saved by God's grace (kindness).

—Ephesians 2:4–5 (ERV)

"For I know the plans I have for you," says the LORD. "They are plans for good and not for disaster, to give you a future and a hope."

—Jeremiah 29:11 (NLT)

No wonder my heart is glad, and my tongue shouts his praises! My body rests in hope. For you will not leave my soul among the dead or allow your Holy One to rot in the grave. You have shown me the way of life, and you will fill me with the joy of your presence.

—Acts 2:26–28 (NLT)

[You have] been born again, not of corruptible seed but incorruptible, through the word of God which lives and abides forever.

—1 Peter 1:23 (NKJV)

I will reward them with a long life and give them my salvation.

—Psalm 91:16 (NLT)

This day I call heaven and earth as witnesses against you that I have set before you life and death, blessings and curses. Now choose life, so that you and your children may live and that you may love the LORD your God, listen to his voice, and hold fast to him. For the LORD is your life, and he will give you many years in the land he swore to give to your fathers, Abraham, Isaac and Jacob.

—Deuteronomy 30:19–20 (NIV)

But now you are free from the power of sin and have become slaves of God. Now you do those things that lead to holiness and result in eternal life. For the wages of sin is death, but the free gift of God is eternal life through Christ Jesus our Lord.

—Romans 6:22–23 (NLT)

And if the Spirit of him who raised Jesus from the dead is living in you, he who raised Christ from the dead will also give life to your mortal bodies through his Spirit, who lives in you.

—Romans 8:11 (NIV)

Some of you were once like that. But you were cleansed; you were made holy; you were made right with God by calling on the name of the Lord Jesus Christ and by the Spirit of our God.

—1 Corinthians 6:11 (NLT)

I pray that the God who gives hope will fill you with much joy and peace while you trust in him. Then you will have more and more hope, and it will flow out of you by the power of the Holy Spirit.

—Romans 15:13 (ERV)

But when the kindness and the love of God our Savior toward man appeared, not by works of righteousness which we have done, but according to His mercy He saved us, through the washing of regeneration and renewing of the Holy Spirit.

—Titus 3:4–5 (NKJV)

Then I will give them one heart, and I will put a new spirit within them, and take the stony heart out of their flesh, and give them a heart of flesh.

—Ezekiel 11:19 (NKJV)

May our Lord Jesus Christ himself and God our Father, who loved us and by his grace gave us eternal encouragement and good hope, encourage your hearts and strengthen you in every good deed and word.

—2 Thessalonians 2:16–17 (NIV)

Praise be to the God and Father of our Lord Jesus Christ. God has great mercy, and because of his mercy he gave us a new life. This new life brings us a living hope through Jesus Christ's rising from death. Now we wait to get the blessings God has for his children. Those blessings are kept for you in heaven. Those blessings cannot ruin or be destroyed or lose their beauty. God's power protects you through your faith, and it keeps you safe until your salvation comes. That salvation is ready to be given to you at the end of time.

—1 Peter 1:3–5 (ERV)

Knowing God RESTORES THE WEARY HEART

Therefore we do not lose heart. Though outwardly we are wasting away, yet inwardly we are being renewed day by day.

—2 Corinthians 4:16 (NIV)

My enemies have set a trap for me. I am ready to give up. But the Lord knows what is happening to me.

—Psalm 142:3 (ERV)

You let me see troubles and bad times. But you saved me from every one of them and kept me alive. No matter how deep I sank, you lifted me out of my troubles. Help me do greater things than before. Continue to comfort me.

—Psalm 71:20–21 (ERV)

The LORD is my shepherd, I shall not be in want. He makes me lie down in green pastures, he leads me beside quiet waters, he restores my soul. He guides me in paths of righteousness for his name's sake.

—Psalm 23:1–3 (NIV)

I am leaving you with a gift—peace of mind and heart. And the peace I give is a gift the world cannot give. So don't be troubled or afraid.

—John 14:27 (NLT)

But You have seen, for You observe trouble and grief, to repay it by Your hand. The helpless commits himself to You; You are the helper of the fatherless.

—Psalm 10:14 (NKJV)

God is our refuge and strength, an ever-present help in trouble.

—Psalm 46:1 (NIV)

Those who live in the shelter of the Most High will find rest in the shadow of the Almighty.

—Psalm 91:1 (NLT)

The Lord my Master gave me the ability to teach. So now I teach these sad people. Every morning he wakes me and teaches me like a student.

—Isaiah 50:4 (ERV)

For in the day of trouble he will keep me safe in his dwelling; he will hide me in the shelter of his tabernacle and set me high upon a rock.

—Psalm 27:5 (NIV)

You, O God, sent a plentiful rain, whereby You confirmed Your inheritance, when it was weary.

—Psalm 68:9 (NKJV)

Pray to the Lord and he will hear you. He will save you from all your troubles.

—Psalm 34:17 (ERV)

Surely you have heard and know that the Lord God is very wise. People can't learn everything he knows. The Lord does not become tired and need to rest. The Lord made all the faraway places on earth. The Lord lives forever.

—Isaiah 40:28 (ERV)

This poor man called, and the LORD heard him; he saved him out of all his troubles.

—Psalm 34:6 (NIV)

The LORD is a shelter for the oppressed, a refuge in times of trouble.

—Psalm 9:9 (NLT)

In the day of my trouble I will call to you, for you will answer me.

—Psalm 86:7 (NIV)

I weep with sorrow; encourage me by your word.

—Psalm 119:28 (NLT)

I will refresh the weary and satisfy the faint.

—Jeremiah 31:25 (NIV)

For thus says the High and Lofty One who inhabits eternity, whose name is Holy: "I dwell in the high and holy place, with him who has a contrite and humble spirit, to revive the spirit of the humble, and to revive the heart of the contrite ones."

—Isaiah 57:15 (NKJV)

God, you are a hiding place for me. You protect me from my troubles. You surround me and protect me. So I sing about the way you saved me.

—Psalm 32:7 (ERV)

Show me Your ways, O Lord; teach me Your paths. Lead me in Your truth and teach me, for You are the God of my salvation; on You I wait all the day.

—Psalm 25:4–5 (NKJV)

Knowing God SUSTAINS YOU

The LORD upholds all who fall, and raises up all who are bowed down.

—Psalm 145:14 (NKJV)

All praise to God, the Father of our Lord Jesus Christ. God is our merciful Father and the source of all comfort. He comforts us in all our troubles so that we can comfort others. When they are troubled, we will be able to give them the same comfort God has given us.

—2 Corinthians 1:3–4 (NLT)

I am a poor, helpless man. God, hurry! Come and save me! God, only you can rescue me. Don't be too late!

—Psalm 70:5 (ERV)

Create in me a clean heart, O God. Renew a loyal spirit within me.

—Psalm 51:10 (NLT)

In his kindness God called you to share in his eternal glory by means of Christ Jesus. So after you have suffered a little while, he will restore, support, and strengthen you, and he will place you on a firm foundation.

—1 Peter 5:10 (NLT)

He gives power to the weak, and to those who have no might He increases strength.

—Isaiah 40:29 (NKJV)

Restore to me the joy of your salvation and grant me a willing spirit, to sustain me.

—Psalm 51:12 (NIV)

A person who respects the Lord has a good life. That person is satisfied with his life and doesn't have to worry about troubles.

—Proverbs 19:23 (ERV)

You hear, O LORD, the desire of the afflicted; you encourage them, and you listen to their cry, defending the fatherless and the oppressed, in order that man, who is of the earth, may terrify no more.

—Psalm 10:17–18 (NIV)

Therefore, having been justified by faith, we have peace with God through our Lord Jesus Christ, through whom also we have access by faith into this grace in which we stand, and rejoice in hope of the glory of God.

—Romans 5:1–2 (NKJV)

Yet I am poor and needy; may the Lord think of me. You are my help and my deliverer; O my God, do not delay.

—Psalm 40:17 (NIV)

We pray that the Lord Jesus Christ himself and God our Father will comfort you and strengthen you in every good thing you do and say. God loved us. Through his grace (kindness) he gave us a good hope and comfort that continues forever.

—2 Thessalonians 2:16–17 (ERV)

I know how to live on almost nothing or with everything. I have learned the secret of living in every situation, whether it is with a full stomach or empty, with plenty or little. For I can do everything through Christ, who gives me strength. Even so, you have done well to share with me in my present difficulty.

—Philippians 4:12–14 (NLT)

Knowing God GIVES YOU A FRESH START

We know that our old sinful selves were crucified with Christ so that sin might lose its power in our lives. We are no longer slaves to sin. For when we died with Christ we were set free from the power of sin.

—*Romans 6:6–7 (NLT)*

But if the Spirit of Him who raised Jesus from the dead dwells in you, He who raised Christ from the dead will also give life to your mortal bodies through His Spirit who dwells in you.

—*Romans 8:11 (NKJV)*

You were dead because of your sins and because your sinful nature was not yet cut away. Then God made you alive with Christ, for he forgave all our sins.

—*Colossians 2:13 (NLT)*

We were therefore buried with him through baptism into death in order that, just as Christ was raised from the dead through the glory of the Father, we too may live a new life.

—Romans 6:4 (NIV)

Praise be to the God and Father of our Lord Jesus Christ. God has great mercy, and because of his mercy he gave us a new life. This new life brings us a living hope through Jesus Christ's rising from death.

—1 Peter 1:3 (ERV)

Jesus said to her, "I am the resurrection and the life. He who believes in Me, though he may die, he shall live. And whoever lives and believes in Me shall never die. Do you believe this?"

—John 11:25–26 (NKJV)

Put off, concerning your former conduct, the old man which grows corrupt according to the deceitful lusts, and be renewed in the spirit of your mind, and that you put on the new man which was created according to God, in true righteousness and holiness.

—*Ephesians 4:22–24 (NKJV)*

Therefore, my brethren, you also have become dead to the law through the body of Christ, that you may be married to another—to Him who was raised from the dead, that we should bear fruit to God.

—*Romans 7:4 (NKJV)*

In the same way, count yourselves dead to sin but alive to God in Christ Jesus.

—*Romans 6:11 (NIV)*

Therefore we do not lose heart. Though outwardly we are wasting away, yet inwardly we are being renewed day by day. For our light and momentary troubles are achieving for us an eternal glory that far outweighs them all.

—2 Corinthians 4:16–17 (NIV)

Turn us again to yourself, O God. Make your face shine down upon us. Only then will we be saved.

—Psalm 80:3 (NLT)

And God raised us up with Christ and gave us a seat with him in the heavenly places. God did this for us who are in Christ Jesus. God did this so that for all future time he could show the very great riches of his grace. God shows that grace by being kind to us in Christ Jesus.

—Ephesians 2:6–7 (ERV)

Christ died, and we have been joined with Christ by dying too. So we will also be joined with him by rising from death like Christ rose from death.

—Romans 6:5 (ERV)

And the God of all grace, who called you to his eternal glory in Christ, after you have suffered a little while, will himself restore you and make you strong, firm and steadfast.

—1 Peter 5:10 (NIV)

D'S PROMIS

ROM

EXPERIENCING

God

[I pray] that you may know what is the hope of His calling, what are the riches of the glory of His inheritance in the saints, and what is the exceeding greatness of His power toward us who believe, according to the working of His mighty power.

—Ephesians 1:18–19 (NKJV)

Trust

Behold, God is my salvation, I will trust and not be afraid; "For YAH, the LORD, is my strength and song; He also has become my salvation."

—Isaiah 12:2 (NKJV)

But blessed are those who trust in the LORD and have made the LORD their hope and confidence. They are like trees planted along a riverbank, with roots that reach deep into the water. Such trees are not bothered by the heat or worried by long months of drought. Their leaves stay green, and they never stop producing fruit.

—Jeremiah 17:7–8 (NLT)

But when I am afraid, I will put my trust in you.

—Psalm 56:3 (NLT)

Those who know your name will trust in you, for you, LORD, have never forsaken those who seek you.

—Psalm 9:10 (NIV)

If a person trusts the Lord, that person will be truly happy. A person will be truly happy if he doesn't turn to demons and false gods for help.

—Psalm 40:4 (ERV)

But I have trusted in Your mercy; my heart shall rejoice in Your salvation.

—Psalm 13:5 (NKJV)

Commit your way to the LORD; trust in him and he will do this: He will make your righteousness shine like the dawn, the justice of your cause like the noonday sun.

—Psalm 37:5–6 (NIV)

To You, O LORD, I lift up my soul. O my God, I trust in You; let me not be ashamed; let not my enemies triumph over me.

—*Psalm 25:1–2 (NKJV)*

The LORD is my strength and my shield; my heart trusts in him, and I am helped. My heart leaps for joy and I will give thanks to him in song.

—*Psalm 28:7 (NIV)*

Many sorrows come to the wicked, but unfailing love surrounds those who trust the LORD.

—*Psalm 32:10 (NLT)*

But I am like a green olive tree in the house of God; I trust in the mercy of God forever and ever.

—*Psalm 52:8 (NKJV)*

Lord, you give true peace to people who depend on you, to people who trust you.

—Isaiah 26:3 (ERV)

In that day the people will proclaim, "This is our God! We trusted in him, and he saved us! This is the Lord, in whom we trusted. Let us rejoice in the salvation he brings!"

—Isaiah 25:9 (NLT)

Let the morning bring me word of your unfailing love, for I have put my trust in you. Show me the way I should go, for to you I lift up my soul.

—Psalm 143:8 (NIV)

But as for me, I trust in You, O Lord; I say, "You are my God."

—Psalm 31:14 (NKJV)

Protect me, for I am devoted to you.
Save me, for I serve you and trust you.
You are my God.

—Psalm 86:2 (NLT)

Fearing people is a dangerous trap, but trusting the LORD means safety.

—Proverbs 29:25 (NLT)

Listen to the things that I say. I will teach you the things wise men have said. Learn from these teachings. It will be good for you if you remember these things. It will help you if you can say these words. I will teach you these things now. I want you to trust the Lord.

—Proverbs 22:17–19 (ERV)

A selfish person causes trouble. But the person who trusts in the Lord will be rewarded.

—Proverbs 28:25 (ERV)

And I will wait on the LORD, Who hides His face from the house of Jacob; and I will hope in Him.

—Isaiah 8:17 (NKJV)

[A good] person will never fall. A good person will be remembered forever. He will not be afraid of bad news. That person is confident because he trusts the Lord.

—Psalm 112:6–7 (ERV)

It is better to take refuge in the LORD than to trust in man.

—Psalm 118:8 (NIV)

For the king trusts in the LORD, and through the mercy of the Most High he shall not be moved.

—Psalm 21:7 (NKJV)

For our heart shall rejoice in Him, because we have trusted in His holy name.

—Psalm 33:21 (NKJV)

In you our fathers put their trust; they trusted and you delivered them. They cried to you and were saved; in you they trusted and were not disappointed.

—Psalm 22:4–5 (NIV)

Yes, the Scripture says, "Any person that trusts in him (Christ) will never be disappointed."

—Romans 10:11 (ERV)

The LORD is good, a refuge in times of trouble. He cares for those who trust in him.

—Nahum 1:7 (NIV)

Trust in the LORD with all your heart; do not depend on your own understanding. Seek his will in all you do, and he will show you which path to take.

—Proverbs 3:5–6 (NLT)

Hope

I pray that God, the source of hope, will fill you completely with joy and peace because you trust in him. Then you will overflow with confident hope through the power of the Holy Spirit.

—Romans 15:13 (NLT)

For everything that was written in the past was written to teach us, so that through endurance and the encouragement of the Scriptures we might have hope.

—Romans 15:4 (NIV)

My soul, wait silently for God alone, for my expectation is from Him.

—Psalm 62:5 (NKJV)

But Job, you should make your heart ready to serve only God, and you should lift up your hands to worship him. . . . Then you would feel safe, because there would be hope. God would care for you and give you rest.

—Job 11:13, 18 (ERV)

And this hope will never disappoint us—it will never fail. Why? Because God has poured out his love to fill our hearts. God gave us his love through the Holy Spirit. That Holy Spirit was a gift to us from God.

—Romans 5:5 (ERV)

You will be rewarded for this; your hope will not be disappointed.

—Proverbs 23:18 (NLT)

So I will look to the Lord for help! I will wait for God to save me. My God will hear me.

—Micah 7:7 (ERV)

But I will keep on hoping for your help; I will praise you more and more.

—Psalm 71:14 (NLT)

But you should keep the Lord Christ holy in your hearts. Always be ready to answer every person who asks you to explain about the hope you have.

—1 Peter 3:15 (ERV)

So shall the knowledge of wisdom be to your soul; if you have found it, there is a prospect, and your hope will not be cut off.

—Proverbs 24:14 (NKJV)

Dear friends, now we are children of God, and what we will be has not yet been made known. But we know that when he appears, we shall be like him, for we shall see him as he is. Everyone who has this hope in him purifies himself, just as he is pure.

—1 John 3:2–3 (NIV)

Remember your promise to me; it is my only hope.

—Psalm 119:49 (NLT)

Sustain me according to your promise, and I will live; do not let my hopes be dashed.

—Psalm 119:116 (NIV)

Guidance

In your unfailing love you will lead the people you have redeemed. In your strength you will guide them to your holy dwelling.

—Exodus 15:13 (NIV)

Guide me and teach me your truths. You are my God, my Savior. I trust you every day.

—Psalm 25:5 (ERV)

When the Spirit of truth comes, he will guide you into all truth. He will not speak on his own but will tell you what he has heard. He will tell you about the future.

—John 16:13 (NLT)

The humble He guides in justice, and the humble He teaches His way.

—Psalm 25:9 (NKJV)

God, you are my Rock, so, for the good of your name, lead me and guide me.

—Psalm 31:3 (ERV)

The integrity of the upright guides them, but the unfaithful are destroyed by their duplicity.

—Proverbs 11:3 (NIV)

The LORD will guide you continually, and satisfy your soul in drought, and strengthen your bones; you shall be like a watered garden, and like a spring of water, whose waters do not fail.

—Isaiah 58:11 (NKJV)

I guide you in the way of wisdom and lead you along straight paths.

—Proverbs 4:11 (NIV)

Lord, if I go east where the sun rises, you are there. If I go west to the sea, you are there. Even there your right hand holds me, and you lead me by the hand.

—Psalm 139:9–10 (ERV)

For you are God, my only safe haven. Why have you tossed me aside? Why must I wander around in grief, oppressed by my enemies? Send out your light and your truth; let them guide me. Let them lead me to your holy mountain, to the place where you live.

—Psalm 43:2–3 (NLT)

For that is what God is like. He is our God forever and ever, and he will guide us until we die.

—Psalm 48:14 (NLT)

God be merciful to us and bless us, and cause His face to shine upon us. . . . Oh, let the nations be glad and sing for joy! For You shall judge the people righteously, and govern the nations on earth.

—*Psalm 67:1, 4 (NKJV)*

Rest

A person who respects the Lord has a good life. That person is satisfied with his life and doesn't have to worry about troubles.

—*Proverbs 19:23 (ERV)*

For thus says the Lord GOD, the Holy One of Israel: "In returning and rest you shall be saved; in quietness and confidence shall be your strength."

—*Isaiah 30:15 (NKJV)*

Moses said this about Benjamin: "The Lord loves Benjamin. Benjamin will live safely near him. The Lord protects him all the time. And the Lord will live in his land."

—*Deuteronomy 33:12 (ERV)*

Then Jesus said, "Come to me, all of you who are weary and carry heavy burdens, and I will give you rest. Take my yoke upon you. Let me teach you, because I am humble and gentle at heart, and you will find rest for your souls. For my yoke is easy to bear, and the burden I give you is light."

—Matthew 11:28–30 (NLT)

Be at rest once more, O my soul, for the LORD has been good to you.

—Psalm 116:7 (NIV)

This shows that the seventh-day rest for God's people is still coming. God rested after he finished his work. So the person who enters and has God's rest is the person who has finished his work like God did.

—Hebrews 4:9–10 (ERV)

The LORD is my shepherd; I shall not want. He makes me to lie down in green pastures; He leads me beside the still waters. He restores my soul; He leads me in the paths of righteousness for His name's sake. Yea, though I walk through the valley of the shadow of death, I will fear no evil; for You are with me; Your rod and Your staff, they comfort me. You prepare a table before me in the presence of my enemies; You anoint my head with oil; my cup runs over. Surely goodness and mercy shall follow me all the days of my life; and I will dwell in the house of the LORD forever.

—Psalm 23:1–6 (NKJV)

My people will live in safety, quietly at home. They will be at rest.

—Isaiah 32:18 (NLT)

My soul finds rest in God alone; my salvation comes from him. He alone is my rock and my salvation; he is my fortress, I will never be shaken. . . . Find rest, O my soul, in God alone; my hope comes from him. He alone is my rock and my salvation; he is my fortress, I will not be shaken. My salvation and my honor depend on God; he is my mighty rock, my refuge. Trust in him at all times, O people; pour out your hearts to him, for God is our refuge. . . . One thing God has spoken, two things have I heard: that you, O God, are strong, and that you, O Lord, are loving. Surely you will reward each person according to what he has done.

—Psalm 62:1–2, 5–8, 11–12 (NIV)

Protection

May the LORD answer you in the day of trouble; may the name of the God of Jacob defend you.

—Psalm 20:1 (NKJV)

"Because he loves me," says the LORD, "I will rescue him; I will protect him, for he acknowledges my name. He will call upon me, and I will answer him; I will be with him in trouble, I will deliver him and honor him."

—Psalm 91:14–15 (NIV)

God is our refuge and strength, always ready to help in times of trouble.

—Psalm 46:1 (NLT)

We wait in hope for the LORD; he is our help and our shield.

—Psalm 33:20 (NIV)

The Lord is good. He is a safe place to go to in times of trouble. He takes care of the people who trust him.

—Nahum 1:7 (ERV)

In peace I will lie down and sleep, for you alone, O LORD, will keep me safe.

—Psalm 4:8 (NLT)

Do not withhold Your tender mercies from me, O LORD; let Your lovingkindness and Your truth continually preserve me.

—Psalm 40:11 (NKJV)

But the Lord is faithful. He will give you strength and protect you from the Evil One (the devil).

—2 Thessalonians 3:3 (ERV)

For the LORD loves the just and will not forsake his faithful ones. They will be protected forever, but the offspring of the wicked will be cut off.

—Psalm 37:28 (NIV)

The Lord says: "You, Israel, are my servant. Jacob, I chose you. You are from Abraham's family. And I loved Abraham. You were in a far away country, but I reached out to you. I called you from that faraway place. I said, 'You are my servant.' I chose you. And I have not rejected you. Don't worry, I am with you. Don't be afraid, I am your God. I will make you strong. I will help you. I will support you with my good right hand. . . . I am the Lord your God. I am holding your right hand. And I tell you: Don't be afraid! I will help you. Precious Judah, don't be afraid! My dear people of Israel, don't be scared! I really will help you." The Lord himself said those things. The Holy One (God) of Israel, the One who saves you, said these things.

—Isaiah 41:8–10, 13–14 (ERV)

For you are my hiding place; you protect me from trouble. You surround me with songs of victory.

—Psalm 32:7 (NLT)

You shall keep them, O LORD, You shall preserve them from this generation forever.

—Psalm 12:7 (NKJV)

God's power is complete. The Lord's word has been tested. He protects people who trust him.

—2 Samuel 22:31 (ERV)

Love

Therefore, as God's chosen people, holy and dearly loved, clothe yourselves with compassion, kindness, humility, gentleness and patience. Bear with each other and forgive whatever grievances you may have against one another. Forgive as the Lord forgave you. And over all these virtues put on love, which binds them all together in perfect unity.

—Colossians 3:12–14 (NIV)

May the Lord make your love increase and overflow for each other and for everyone else, just as ours does for you.

—1 Thessalonians 3:12 (NIV)

Your love for one another will prove to the world that you are my disciples.

—John 13:35 (NLT)

But we don't need to write to you about the importance of loving each other, for God himself has taught you to love one another. Indeed, you already show your love for all the believers throughout Macedonia. Even so, dear brothers and sisters, we urge you to love them even more.

—1 Thessalonians 4:9–10 (NLT)

Their hearts may be encouraged, being knit together in love, and attaining to all riches of the full assurance of understanding, to the knowledge of the mystery of God, both of the Father and of Christ, in whom are hidden all the treasures of wisdom and knowledge.

—Colossians 2:2–3 (NKJV)

Beloved, let us love one another, for love is of God; and everyone who loves is born of God and knows God.

—1 John 4:7 (NKJV)

I may speak in different languages of men or even angels. But if I don't have love, then I am only a noisy bell or a ringing cymbal. I may have the gift of prophecy; I may understand all the secret things of God and know everything; and I may have faith so great that I can move mountains. But even with all these things, if I don't have love, then I am nothing. I may give everything I have to feed people. And I may even give my body as an offering to be burned. But I gain nothing by doing these things if I don't have love. Love is patient, and love is kind. Love is not jealous, it does not boast, and it is not proud. Love is not rude, love is not selfish, and love does not become angry easily. Love does not remember wrongs done against it. Love is not happy with evil, but love is happy with the truth. Love patiently accepts all things. Love always trusts, always hopes, and always continues strong. Love never ends. There are gifts of prophecy, but they will be ended. There are gifts of speaking in different kinds of languages, but those gifts will end. There is the gift of knowledge, but it will be ended.

—1 Corinthians 13:1–8 (ERV)

But I tell you, love your enemies. Pray for those people that do bad things to you. If you do this, then you will be true sons of your Father in heaven. Your Father lets the sun rise for the good people and the bad people. Your Father sends rain to people that do good and to people that do wrong.

—Matthew 5:44–45 (ERV)

Joy

For You, LORD, have made me glad through Your work; I will triumph in the works of Your hands.

—Psalm 92:4 (NKJV)

I pray that the God who gives hope will fill you with much joy and peace while you trust in him. Then you will have more and more hope, and it will flow out of you by the power of the Holy Spirit.

—Romans 15:13 (ERV)

Restore to me the joy of your salvation, and make me willing to obey you.

—Psalm 51:12 (NLT)

The LORD has done great things for us, and we are filled with joy.

—Psalm 126:3 (NIV)

The hope of the righteous will be gladness, but the expectation of the wicked will perish.

—Proverbs 10:28 (NKJV)

But the Holy Spirit produces this kind of fruit in our lives: love, joy, peace, patience, kindness, goodness, faithfulness, gentleness, and self-control. There is no law against these things!

—Galatians 5:22–23 (NLT)

Consider it pure joy, my brothers, whenever you face trials of many kinds, because you know that the testing of your faith develops perseverance.

—James 1:2–3 (NIV)

In the kingdom of God, eating and drinking are not important. In the kingdom of God, the important things are these: living right with God, peace, and joy in the Holy Spirit. Any person who serves Christ by living this way is pleasing God. And that person will be accepted by other people.

—Romans 14:17–18 (ERV)

Though now you do not see Him, yet believing, you rejoice with joy inexpressible and full of glory, receiving the end of your faith—the salvation of your souls.

—1 Peter 1:8–9 (NKJV)

You have loved righteousness and hated lawlessness; therefore God, Your God, has anointed You with the oil of gladness more than Your companions.

—Hebrews 1:9 (NKJV)

I am coming to you now. But I pray these things while I am still in the world. I say these things so that these men can have the true happiness that I have. I want them to be completely happy.

—John 17:13 (ERV)

Now all glory to God, who is able to keep you from falling away and will bring you with great joy into his glorious presence without a single fault. All glory to him who alone is God, our Savior through Jesus Christ our Lord. All glory, majesty, power, and authority are his before all time, and in the present, and beyond all time! Amen.

—Jude 24–25 (NLT)

For a day in Your courts is better than a thousand. I would rather be a doorkeeper in the house of my God than dwell in the tents of wickedness.

—Psalm 84:10 (NKJV)

Walk in all the way that the Lord your God has commanded you, so that you may live and prosper and prolong your days in the land that you will possess.

—Deuteronomy 5:33 (NIV)

In the past he permitted all the nations to go their own ways, but he never left them without evidence of himself and his goodness. For instance, he sends you rain and good crops and gives you food and joyful hearts.

—Acts 14:16–17 (NLT)

I am overwhelmed with joy in the Lord my God! For he has dressed me with the clothing of salvation and draped me in a robe of righteousness. I am like a bridegroom in his wedding suit or a bride with her jewels.

—Isaiah 61:10 (NLT)

You will teach me the right way to live. Just being with you, Lord, will bring complete happiness. Being at your right side will bring happiness forever.

—Psalm 16:11 (ERV)

Peace

Therefore, since we have been made right in God's sight by faith, we have peace with God because of what Jesus Christ our Lord has done for us.

—Romans 5:1 (NLT)

May the God of hope fill you with all joy and peace as you trust in him, so that you may overflow with hope by the power of the Holy Spirit.

—Romans 15:13 (NIV)

Finally, brethren, farewell. Become complete. Be of good comfort, be of one mind, live in peace; and the God of love and peace will be with you.

—2 Corinthians 13:11 (NKJV)

God blesses those who work for peace, for they will be called the children of God.

—Matthew 5:9 (NLT)

And God's peace will keep your hearts and minds in Christ Jesus. That peace which God gives is so great that we cannot understand it.

—Philippians 4:7 (ERV)

But the wisdom that is from above is first pure, then peaceable, gentle, willing to yield, full of mercy and good fruits, without partiality and without hypocrisy. Now the fruit of righteousness is sown in peace by those who make peace.

—James 3:17–18 (NKJV)

When people's lives please the LORD, even their enemies are at peace with them.

—Proverbs 16:7 (NLT)

The LORD bless you and keep you; the LORD make His face shine upon you, and be gracious to you; the LORD lift up His countenance upon you, and give you peace.

—Numbers 6:24–26 (NKJV)

The LORD gives strength to his people; the LORD blesses his people with peace.

—Psalm 29:11 (NIV)

Now may the God of peace Himself sanctify you completely; and may your whole spirit, soul, and body be preserved blameless at the coming of our Lord Jesus Christ.

—1 Thessalonians 5:23 (NKJV)

Grace (kindness) and peace be given to you more and more, because now you know God and Jesus our Lord.

—2 Peter 1:2 (ERV)

May the God of peace, who through the blood of the eternal covenant brought back from the dead our Lord Jesus, that great Shepherd of the sheep, equip you with everything good for doing his will, and may he work in us what is pleasing to him, through Jesus Christ, to whom be glory for ever and ever. Amen.

—Hebrews 13:20–21 (NIV)

Worship

The LORD lives! Praise to my Rock! May the God of my salvation be exalted!

—Psalm 18:46 (NLT)

Come, let us bow down in worship, let us kneel before the LORD our Maker.

—Psalm 95:6 (NIV)

Then Moses and the people of Israel sang this song to the LORD: "I will sing to the LORD, for he has triumphed gloriously; he has hurled both horse and rider into the sea. The LORD is my strength and my song; he has given me victory. This is my God, and I will praise him—my father's God, and I will exalt him!"

—Exodus 15:1–2 (NLT)

Lord, you are my God and I thank you. I praise you!

—Psalm 118:28 (ERV)

By You I have been upheld from birth; You are He who took me out of my mother's womb. My praise shall be continually of You.

—Psalm 71:6 (NKJV)

All praise to God, the Father of our Lord Jesus Christ, who has blessed us with every spiritual blessing in the heavenly realms because we are united with Christ.

—Ephesians 1:3 (NLT)

Praise be to the God and Father of our Lord Jesus Christ. God has great mercy, and because of his mercy he gave us a new life. This new life brings us a living hope through Jesus Christ's rising from death.

—1 Peter 1:3 (ERV)

I praise you because I am fearfully and wonderfully made; your works are wonderful, I know that full well.

—Psalm 139:14 (NIV)

Great is the Lord! He is most worthy of praise! He is to be feared above all gods.

—1 Chronicles 16:25 (NLT)

The Lord lives! Blessed be my Rock! Let God be exalted, the Rock of my salvation!

—2 Samuel 22:47 (NKJV)

Be exalted, O God, above the heavens; let your glory be over all the earth.

—Psalm 57:5 (NIV)

Lord Most-High, you really are the ruler of the earth. You are much better than the "gods."

—Psalm 97:9 (ERV)

Blessed be the LORD God of Israel from everlasting to everlasting! And all the people said, "Amen!" and praised the LORD.

—1 Chronicles 16:36 (NKJV)

I praise the Lord with all my heart. Lord, I will tell about all the wonderful things you did. You make me so very happy. God Most-High, I praise your name.

—Psalm 9:1–2 (ERV)

Praise the LORD! For he has heard my cry for mercy.

—Psalm 28:6 (NLT)

Lord, you lifted me up out of my troubles. You did not let my enemies defeat me and laugh at me. So I will show honor to you.

—Psalm 30:1 (ERV)

Praise be to the LORD, for he showed his wonderful love to me when I was in a besieged city.

—Psalm 31:21 (NIV)

Rejoice in the LORD, O you righteous! For praise from the upright is beautiful.

—Psalm 33:1 (NKJV)

I bless the Lord all the time. His praise is always on my lips.

—Psalm 34:1 (ERV)

Come, let us tell of the LORD's greatness; let us exalt his name together.

—Psalm 34:3 (NLT)

Why are you cast down, O my soul? And why are you disquieted within me? Hope in God; for I shall yet praise Him, the help of my countenance and my God.

—Psalm 42:11 (NKJV)

Bless the LORD, O my soul; and all that is within me, bless His holy name! Bless the LORD, O my soul, and forget not all His benefits.

—Psalm 103:1–2 (NKJV)

Praise the LORD! Praise God in his sanctuary; praise him in his mighty heaven! Praise him for his mighty works; praise his unequaled greatness! . . . Let everything that breathes sing praises to the LORD! Praise the LORD!

—Psalm 150:1–2, 6 (NLT)

I will bow down toward your holy temple and will praise your name for your love and your faithfulness, for you have exalted above all things your name and your word.

—Psalm 138:2 (NIV)

They sang, “Amen! Blessing and glory and wisdom and thanksgiving and honor and power and strength belong to our God forever and ever! Amen.”

—*Revelation 7:12 (NLT)*

Other TITLES TO ENJOY IN THIS SERIES INCLUDE:

GOD'S PROMISES ON HEALING
GOD'S PROMISES ON PRAISE AND WORSHIP
GOD'S PROMISES ON CHARACTER
GOD'S PROMISES ON PRAYER
GOD'S PROMISES ON HIS LOVE
GOD'S PROMISES ON SIMPLICITY
GOD'S PROMISES ON THE FRUIT OF THE SPIRIT

GOD'S PROMISES GOD'S PROMISES GOD'S PR